This journal belongs to:

....

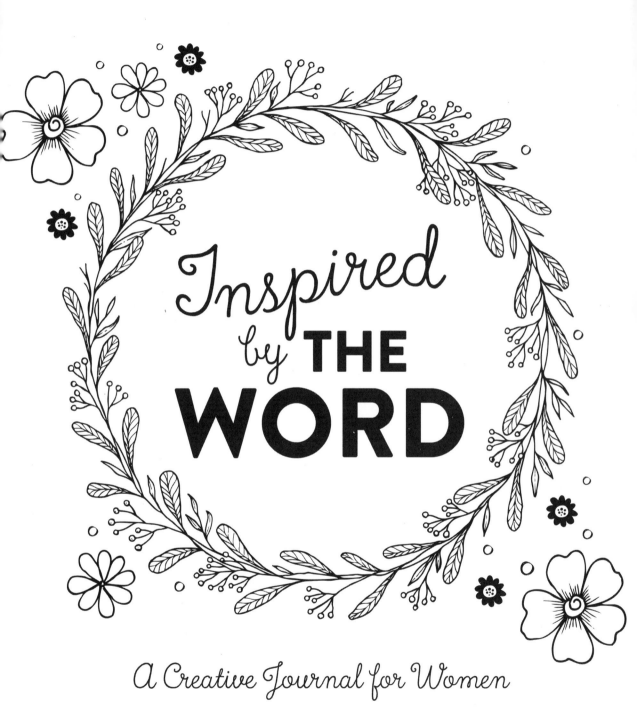

Inspired by THE WORD

A Creative Journal for Women

BARBOUR BOOKS
An Imprint of Barbour Publishing, Inc.

ISBN 978-1-68322-710-6

Journal prompts written by Shanna D. Gregor.

Scripture quotations are taken from the King James Version of the Bible.

Published by Barbour Books, an imprint of Barbour Publishing, Inc., 1810 Barbour Drive, Uhrichsville, Ohio 44683, www.barbourbooks.com

Our mission is to inspire the world with the life-changing message of the Bible.

Member of the
Evangelical Christian
Publishers Association

Printed in China.

Introduction

Be inspired by "The Word" with this lovely creative journal!
 Delightful word art to color and encouraging scripture passages from the beloved King James Version of the Bible, plus thought-provoking journal prompts and generous room to write will inspire you to grow in your faith as you spend quiet time in your heavenly Creator's presence.
 One hundred inspiring words—including Peace, Wonder, Miracles, Heaven, Purpose, Celebrate, and more—will inspire you to think more deeply on God and His promise-filled Word.

In the beginning was the Word, and the Word was with God, and the Word was God.

JOHN 1:1

Be of good courage, and he shall strengthen
your heart, all ye that hope in the LORD.

PSALM 31:24

What gives you courage?

And ye shall know the truth,
and the truth shall make you free.

John 8:32

....
....
....
....
....
....
....
....
....
....
....
....
....
....
....

How has God's truth made you free?

Whosoever believeth in him
should not perish, but have eternal life.

JOHN 3:15

....
....
....
....
....

What does it mean to you to know you have eternal life?

Enter into his gates with thanksgiving, and into his courts
with praise: be thankful unto him, and bless his name.

PSALM 100:4

....
....
....
....
....

Write down your thoughts on praising God's name.

But the fruit of the Spirit is love, joy,
peace, longsuffering, gentleness, goodness, faith. . .

GALATIANS 5:22

....
....
....
....
....
....
....
....
....
....
....

Write about a time when you showed love to someone, even though you may not have "felt" like loving that person.

....

....

....

....

....

....

....

....

....

....

....

....

....

....

....

....

....

....

....

....

....

....

....

Blessings are upon the head of the just.

PROVERBS 10:6

....

....

....

....

....

....

Christ has justified you by way of the cross. What blessings have you experienced lately?

....

....

....

....

....

....

....

....

....

....

....

....

....

....

....

....

....

....

....

....

....

....

....

....

In the morning will I direct
my prayer unto thee, and will look up.

PSALM 5:3

....

....

....

....

....

....

....

....

....

....

....

....

What is your prayer today? (Revisit this entry at a later date, and then record how God answers.)

....
....
....
....
....
....
....
....
....
....
....
....
....
....
....
....
....
....
....
....
....
....
....

Now faith is the substance of things hoped for,
the evidence of things not seen.

HEBREWS 11:1

Write about a time you believed *before* seeing the result of your faith.

. . . .

. . . .

. . . .

. . . .

. . . .

. . . .

. . . .

. . . .

. . . .

. . . .

. . . .

. . . .

. . . .

. . . .

. . . .

. . . .

. . . .

. . . .

. . . .

. . . .

. . . .

. . . .

. . . .

Rejoice ye in that day, and leap for joy: for,
behold, your reward is great in heaven.

LUKE 6:23

....
....
....
....
....
....

How does it make you feel to know that you will receive rewards in heaven?

....

....

....

....

....

....

....

....

....

....

....

....

....

....

....

....

....

....

....

....

....

....

And my soul shall be joyful in
the LORD: it shall rejoice in his salvation.

PSALM 35:9

....
....
....
....
....
....
....
....
....
....
....

What makes joy bubble over in your heart?

God loveth a cheerful giver.

2 CORINTHIANS 9:7

Do you love to give? Why or why not?

Then was our mouth filled with laughter,
and our tongue with singing.

<small>PSALM 126:2</small>

....

....

....

....

....

....

Sometimes we become so busy with life that we forget to enjoy it. What do you enjoy most about your life?

....

....

....

....

....

....

....

....

....

....

....

....

....

....

....

....

....

....

....

....

....

....

My grace is sufficient for thee:
for my strength is made perfect in weakness.

2 Corinthians 12:9

Write about a time you felt weak, but also knew God infused you with His strength.

Worship the LORD in the beauty of holiness.

PSALM 29:2

....

....

....

....

....

....

....

How often do you worship, and what does worship look like for you?

....
....
....
....
....
....
....
....
....
....
....
....
....
....
....
....
....
....
....
....
....
....

For whatsoever things were written aforetime were written for our learning, that we through patience and comfort of the scriptures might have hope.

ROMANS 15:4

What scripture most inspires your soul?

....

....

....

....

....

....

....

....

....

....

....

....

....

....

....

....

....

....

....

....

....

....

....

Trust in the LORD with all thine heart;
and lean not unto thine own understanding.

PROVERBS 3:5

....
....
....
....
....
....
....
....
....
....
....
....
....
....

When you struggle to trust, what helps you hold tighter to
Christ?

....

....

....

....

....

....

....

....

....

....

....

....

....

....

....

....

....

....

....

....

....

....

....

For his merciful kindness is great toward us:
and the truth of the LORD endureth for ever.

PSALM 117:2

....

....

....

....

....

....

How has God shown you His kindness this week?

The LORD is my strength and song,
and he is become my salvation.

EXODUS 15:2

....

....

....

....

....

....

God saves us from many things. Write about something
unexpected that you have received as a result of your salvation.

....

....

....

....

....

....

....

....

....

....

....

....

....

....

....

....

....

....

....

....

....

....

For by grace are ye saved through faith.

EPHESIANS 2:8

....
....
....
....
....
....
....
....
....
....
....
....
....
....
....
....

When have you shown someone else grace? How did it make you feel?

But godliness with contentment is great gain.

1 Timothy 6:6

It's human to want more at times. How do you find contentment with what you have?

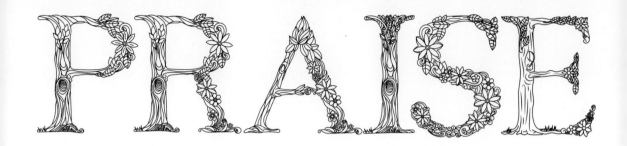

I will praise thee, O LORD, with my whole heart.

PSALM 9:1

What does it mean to give your whole heart to Christ?

For he remembered his holy promise.

PSALM 105:42

....
....
....
....
....
....

What promise has God fulfilled in your life?

But the meek shall inherit the earth;
and shall delight themselves in the abundance of peace.

Psalm 37:11

....

....

....

....

....

....

....

....

....

....

....

....

....

....

When have you chosen to respond gently to something hurtful?
What fruit did that produce in your life?

I will remember the works of the LORD:
surely I will remember thy wonders of old.

PSALM 77:11

....
....
....
....
....

What works of the Lord are special to you?

No man can do these miracles that
thou doest, except God be with him.

JOHN 3:2

Write about a time you thought something was a coincidence at first, only to realize it was a miracle instead.

CREATE

In the beginning God created the heaven and the earth.

GENESIS 1:1

You are a created being with the DNA of God inside you. What has God called you to create in your life?

....

....

....

....

....

....

....

....

....

....

....

....

....

....

....

....

....

....

....

....

....

....

....

INSPIRE

My heart standeth in awe of thy word.

PSALM 119:161

....
....
....
....
....
....
....
....
....
....
....
....
....
....
....
....

Think about the last truth God revealed to you in His Word. How did it impact your heart and life?

He maketh the storm a calm.

PSALM 107:29

Sometimes the storm rages within our spirits. How does the Lord calm the storm inside of you?

....
....
....
....
....
....
....
....
....
....
....
....
....
....
....
....
....
....
....
....
....
....

Trust in. . .the living God, who
giveth us richly all things to enjoy.

1 Timothy 6:17

Have you ever received a gift from God that you've truly enjoyed?

In my Father's house are many mansions: if it were not so,
I would have told you. I go to prepare a place for you. And if
I go and prepare a place for you, I will come again, and receive
you unto myself; that where I am, there ye may be also.

JOHN 14:2-3

....

....

....

....

....

....

....

....

....

....

....

What does "home" mean to you?

And now, Lord, what wait I for? my hope is in thee.

PSALM 39:7

What God-given dream have you put on a shelf? Or what dream is God working to bring to fruition in you?

....
....
....
....
....
....
....
....
....
....
....
....
....
....
....
....
....
....
....
....
....
....

It was meet that we should make merry,
and be glad: for this thy brother was dead,
and is alive again; and was lost, and is found.

LUKE 15:32

....

....

....

....

....

What do you need to celebrate this week? How will you celebrate it?

But thou. . .follow after righteousness,
godliness, faith, love, patience, meekness.

1 TIMOTHY 6:11

God created us to win at life. When you get knocked down, what compels you to get back up and try again?

....
....
....
....
....
....
....
....
....
....
....
....
....
....
....
....
....
....
....
....
....
....
....

But lay up for yourselves treasures in heaven,
where neither moth nor rust doth corrupt,
and where thieves do not break through nor steal.

MATTHEW 6:20

What things are most precious to you?

....

....

....

....

....

....

....

....

....

....

....

....

....

....

....

....

....

....

....

....

....

Whatsoever things are true, whatsoever things are honest, whatsoever things are just, whatsoever things are pure, whatsoever things are lovely, whatsoever things are of good report; if there be any virtue, and if there be any praise, think on these things.

PHILIPPIANS 4:8

Share a favorite memory here.

Now unto him that is able to do exceeding abundantly above all that we ask or think, according to the power that worketh in us, Unto him be glory in the church by Christ Jesus throughout all ages, world without end. Amen.

EPHESIANS 3:20-21

Whatever you can imagine, God can exceed it. Write about a big dream in your heart.

....
....
....
....
....
....
....
....
....
....
....
....
....
....
....
....
....
....
....
....
....
....
....
....

I will praise thee; for I am fearfully and wonderfully made:
marvellous are thy works; and that my soul knoweth right well.

PSALM 139:14

....
....
....
....
....
....
....
....
....
....
....
....
....

God created you to be different from everyone else. How do you celebrate your uniqueness?

_____

_____

_____

_____

_____

_____

_____

_____

_____

_____

_____

_____

_____

_____

_____

_____

_____

_____

_____

_____

_____

_____

_____

_____

_____

And whatsoever ye do, do it heartily,
as to the Lord, and not unto men.

COLOSSIANS 3:23

Are you a loyal person? How has loyalty played a part in your life?

....
....
....
....
....
....
....
....
....
....
....
....
....
....
....
....
....
....
....
....
....
....
....
....
....

In the fear of the LORD is strong confidence.

PROVERBS 14:26

....

....

....

....

....

....

....

How has God used a particular circumstance to build your confidence in Him?

And Jesus went about all the cities and villages, teaching
in their synagogues, and preaching the gospel of the kingdom,
and healing every sickness and every disease among the people.

MATTHEW 9:35

....

....

....

....

Have you experienced healing in your body or in your heart?

And we know that all things work together for good to them that love God, to them who are the called according to his purpose.

ROMANS 8:28

How has God turned something you considered bad into something used for your good?

....

....

....

....

....

....

....

....

....

....

....

....

....

....

....

....

....

....

....

....

....

....

....

With men this is impossible;
but with God all things are possible.

MATTHEW 19:26

....
....
....
....
....

How has God's miraculous power surprised you?

For my yoke is easy, and my burden is light.

MATTHEW 11:30

....

....

....

....

....

....

....

Think about a situation that seems complicated and take a step back. How can you see it differently—more simply? Ask God to help you.

....
....
....
....
....
....
....
....
....
....
....
....
....
....
....
....
....
....
....
....
....
....
....
....
....

Every man according as he purposeth in his heart,
so let him give; not grudgingly, or of necessity:
for God loveth a cheerful giver.

2 Corinthians 9:7

Write about a time you gave generously. How did it make you feel?

Why art thou cast down, O my soul? and why art thou
disquieted within me? hope thou in God: for I shall yet praise
him, who is the health of my countenance, and my God.

PSALM 42:11

What are you expecting from God today?

Every devoted thing is most holy unto the LORD.

LEVITICUS 27:28

....

....

....

....

....

....

....

Many believe that what's most important to you is revealed by where you give most of your time. From this perspective, what would you say you are most devoted to?

O love the LORD, all ye his saints: for the LORD preserveth
the faithful, and plentifully rewardeth the proud doer.

PSALM 31:23

....

....

....

....

....

....

What have you received from God that you would consider a reward?

....

....

....

....

....

....

....

....

....

....

....

....

....

....

....

....

....

....

....

....

....

....

....

....

But thou, O Lord, art a God full of compassion, and gracious, long suffering, and plenteous in mercy and truth.

PSALM 86:15

Discuss the fruit that you believe others would say is most visible in your life.

··

··

··

··

··

··

··

··

··

··

··

··

··

··

··

··

··

··

··

··

··

··

··

··

The LORD God, merciful and gracious,
longsuffering, and abundant in goodness and truth. . .

EXODUS 34:6

What does an abundant life look like to you?

Glory ye in his holy name:
let the heart of them rejoice that seek the LORD.

1 Chronicles 16:10

....
....
....
....
....
....

Choose something you are rejoicing over and write about that experience.

....
....
....
....
....
....
....
....
....
....
....
....
....
....
....
....
....
....
....
....
....
....
....
....
....

Trust in him at all times; ye people,
pour out your heart before him: God is a refuge for us.

PSALM 62:8

....

....

....

....

....

....

How and when has God been your refuge?

Worthy is the Lamb that was slain to receive power, and riches, and wisdom, and strength, and honour, and glory, and blessing.

REVELATION 5:12

Through Christ's sacrifice, He made you worthy. How does that make you feel?

....
....
....
....
....
....
....
....
....
....
....
....
....
....
....
....
....
....
....
....
....
....
....
....
....

These things I have spoken unto you, that in me ye might have peace. In the world ye shall have tribulation: but be of good cheer; I have overcome the world.

JOHN 16:33

....
....
....
....
....

Write about a time when you found yourself comforted and at peace even with trouble around you.

....

....

....

....

....

....

....

....

....

....

....

....

....

....

....

....

....

....

....

....

....

I am the light of the world: he that followeth me shall not walk in darkness, but shall have the light of life.

JOHN 8:12

....
....
....
....
....
....
....
....
....
....
....
....
....

When has someone else's life shined brightly for God and influenced your life?

GIFT

If ye then, being evil, know how to give good gifts unto your children, how much more shall your Father which is in heaven give good things to them that ask him?

MATTHEW 7:11

....
....
....
....
....
....
....
....
....
....
....
....
....

Aside from salvation, what other gifts has God bestowed on you?
Write about one here or make a list.

....
....
....
....
....
....
....
....
....
....
....
....
....
....
....
....
....
....
....
....
....
....
....
....

Humble yourselves in the sight of the Lord,
and he shall lift you up.

JAMES 4:10

Write about a time when you chose humility and God honored you for it.

Fear ye not therefore, ye are of more value than many sparrows.

MATTHEW 10:31

....

....

....

....

....

....

....

....

....

....

....

....

....

....

....

....

How does your value in God's eyes versus the world's perspective make you feel about yourself and your relationship with Him?

O sing unto the LORD a new song: sing unto the LORD,
all the earth. Sing unto the LORD, bless his name.

PSALM 96:1-2

....

....

....

....

....

....

....

....

....

....

....

....

....

....

Sometimes an encouraging song from long ago comes to mind. What was the last worship song that popped into your head, and what did it do for you in that moment?

....
....
....
....
....
....
....
....
....
....
....
....
....
....
....
....
....
....
....
....
....
....
....
....
....
....
....
....
....
....
....
....

Give thanks unto the LORD, call upon his name,
make known his deeds among the people.

1 CHRONICLES 16:8

When was the last time you shared the good that God is doing in your life? Write about that interaction here.

To the praise of the glory of his grace, wherein
he hath made us accepted in the beloved.

EPHESIANS 1:6

....

....

....

....

....

....

What does it mean to you to know that you have God's love and acceptance?

....
....
....
....
....
....
....
....
....
....
....
....
....
....
....
....
....
....
....
....
....
....
....

Thanks be to God, which giveth us the
victory through our Lord Jesus Christ.

1 Corinthians 15:57

....
....
....
....
....
....

Write about a recent victory that you know only happened because of God's intervention.

....
....
....
....
....
....
....
....
....
....
....
....
....
....
....
....
....
....
....
....
....
....
....

I delight to do thy will, O my God:
yea, thy law is within my heart.

PSALM 40:8

How do God's commands lead and direct your life?

....

....

....

....

....

....

....

....

....

....

....

....

....

....

....

....

....

....

....

....

....

....

....

....

....

The LORD hath done that which he had devised; he hath fulfilled
his word that he had commanded in the days of old.

LAMENTATIONS 2:17

....
....
....
....
....
....

God keeps His promises. Give an example of how you make it a priority to keep your own promises.

....

....

....

....

....

....

....

....

....

....

....

....

....

....

....

....

....

....

....

....

....

....

....

....

I will praise thee, O LORD, with my whole heart;
I will shew forth all thy marvellous works.

PSALM 9:1

....
....
....
....
....
....
....
....
....
....
....
....
....
....
....

Write about the last time you truly gave your whole heart in praise.

....

....

....

....

....

....

....

....

....

....

....

....

....

....

....

....

....

....

....

....

....

....

Making request, if by any means now at length I might have
a prosperous journey by the will of God to come unto you.

ROMANS 1:10

....

....

....

....

....

....

....

How have those you've met on your journey of faith influenced
you for God's glory?

....

....

....

....

....

....

....

....

....

....

....

....

....

....

....

....

....

....

....

....

....

....

O LORD, our Lord, how excellent is thy name in all the earth!
who hast set thy glory above the heavens.

PSALM 8:1

Share about a time when you've given God glory. What do you think His response was in that moment?

My soul followeth hard after thee: thy right hand upholdeth me.

PSALM 63:8

Are there times when you find it difficult to surrender all to God? Write about one of those times and how you feel about it now, looking back.

For the Lamb which is in the midst of the throne shall feed them, and shall lead them unto living fountains of waters.

REVELATION 7:17

....

....

....

....

....

....

Without water, we eventually die. How have the living waters of God provided for you this past week?

....
....
....
....
....
....
....
....
....
....
....
....
....
....
....
....
....
....
....
....
....
....
....

Every word of God is pure: he is a shield unto them that put their trust in him.

PROVERBS 30:5

....
....
....
....
....
....
....
....
....
....
....
....
....
....

How has your trust in the Lord grown as you've studied the truths in His Word?

Good and upright is the LORD.

PSALM 25:8

Was there ever a season when you felt like God wasn't good?
How were your eyes opened to see His goodness?

Be still, and know that I am God.

PSALM 46:10

....
....
....
....
....
....
....

Why do you think "being still" is so hard sometimes?

If thou shalt confess with thy mouth the Lord Jesus, and shalt believe in thine heart that God hath raised him from the dead, thou shalt be saved.

ROMANS 10:9

Besides eternal damnation, what else have you been saved from?

For therein is the righteousness of God revealed from faith to faith: as it is written, The just shall live by faith.

ROMANS 1:17

What does it mean to you to know you are the "righteousness of God" in Christ Jesus?

....

....

....

....

....

....

....

....

....

....

....

....

....

....

....

....

....

....

....

....

....

....

....

....

And thou shalt be secure, because there is hope.

JOB 11:18

....

....

....

....

....

....

....

....

When do you feel most secure?

Repent ye therefore, and be converted, that your sins
may be blotted out, when the times of refreshing
shall come from the presence of the Lord.

ACTS 3:19

....
....
....
....
....

Share about a wonderful time of refreshment you have had with the Lord.

Surely goodness and mercy shall follow me all the days of my life: and I will dwell in the house of the LORD for ever.

PSALM 23:6

Is it easy for you to show others mercy? Why or why not?

Stand fast therefore in the liberty wherewith Christ hath made us free, and be not entangled again with the yoke of bondage.

GALATIANS 5:1

In what way have you experienced freedom because of your relationship with God?

....
....
....
....
....
....
....
....
....
....
....
....
....
....
....
....
....
....
....
....
....
....
....
....

He that followeth after righteousness and
mercy findeth life, righteousness, and honour.

PROVERBS 21:21

What keeps you on track to continue following God's lead?

Confess your faults one to another,
and pray one for another, that ye may be healed.

JAMES 5:16

....
....
....
....
....
....

Do you share things with people you trust? How do you feel after your conversation?

....
....
....
....
....
....
....
....
....
....
....
....
....
....
....
....
....
....
....
....
....
....
....
....
....

As snow in summer, and as rain in harvest,
so honour is not seemly for a fool.

PROVERBS 26:1

....

....

....

....

....

....

What are some seeds you've recently planted in your life that you are expecting to receive a harvest from?

....

....

....

....

....

....

....

....

....

....

....

....

....

....

....

....

....

....

....

....

....

....

For as he thinketh in his heart, so is he.

PROVERBS 23:7

....

....

....

....

....

....

....

What do you find yourself thinking about most? How do your thoughts affect your life?

....
....
....
....
....
....
....
....
....
....
....
....
....
....
....
....
....
....
....
....
....
....
....
....
....
....
....

Blessed are they whose iniquities are forgiven,
and whose sins are covered.

ROMANS 4:7

....
....
....
....
....
....

Is there anyone in your life that you need to forgive? What conversations do you need to have with the Lord or with that person before you can truly forgive?

....

....

....

....

....

....

....

....

....

....

....

....

....

....

....

....

....

....

....

....

....

....

Honour thy father and mother;
which is the first commandment with promise.

EPHESIANS 6:2

....
....
....
....
....
....
....
....
....
....
....
....
....
....
....
....

How have you honored your father and/or mother?

Obey my voice, and I will be your God,
and ye shall be my people.

JEREMIAH 7:23

....

....

....

....

....

....

Think of a time when you obeyed God. How did obedience bring blessing into your life?

....

....

....

....

....

....

....

....

....

....

....

....

....

....

....

....

....

....

....

....

....

....

....

....

Looking unto Jesus the author and finisher of our faith; who for the joy that was set before him endured the cross, despising the shame, and is set down at the right hand of the throne of God.

Hebrews 12:2

....
....
....
....
....
....
....
....
....
....
....
....
....

How does your relationship with the Lord help you to stay focused on His purpose for your life?

....

....

....

....

....

....

....

....

....

....

....

....

....

....

....

....

....

....

....

....

....

Be not forgetful to entertain strangers:
for thereby some have entertained angels unawares.

HEBREWS 13:2

....
....
....
....
....
....

Write about a time you possibly encountered an angel, or when angels may have intervened to keep you from harm.

....
....
....
....
....
....
....
....
....
....
....
....
....
....
....
....
....
....
....
....
....
....
....
....
....
....

That if thou shalt confess with thy mouth the Lord Jesus,
and shalt believe in thine heart that God hath raised
him from the dead, thou shalt be saved.

ROMANS 10:9

Do you find some things easier to believe than others when it comes to your faith journey? What comes easy? What is more difficult? Why?

....
....
....
....
....
....
....
....
....
....
....
....
....
....
....
....
....
....
....
....
....

Blessed is the nation whose God is the LORD; and the people whom he hath chosen for his own inheritance.

PSALM 33:12

....
....
....
....
....
....

Do you pray for your nation? What are some of your weightiest concerns?

Pleasant words are as an honeycomb,
sweet to the soul, and health to the bones.

PROVERBS 16:24

What are some of the things you do to help you choose sweet and pleasant words, especially in the midst of frustration with those you love most?

....

....

....

....

....

....

....

....

....

....

....

....

....

....

....

....

....

....

....

....

....

....

The righteous shall flourish like the palm tree:
he shall grow like a cedar in Lebanon.

PSALM 92:12

....
....
....
....
....
....
....
....
....
....
....
....
....
....

Helping others grow in their faith is both challenging and rewarding. Write about a past experience in which you shared your faith.

....

....

....

....

....

....

....

....

....

....

....

....

....

....

....

....

....

....

....

....

....

....

....

O the depth of the riches both of the
wisdom and knowledge of God!

ROMANS 11:33

Who in your life do you go to for wisdom? Why?

When he, the Spirit of truth,
is come, he will guide you into all truth.

John 16:13

....
....
....
....
....
....
....
....
....
....
....
....
....
....

The Bible says that the sheep know their shepherd's voice. What are some of the ways the Shepherd speaks to you?

....
....
....
....
....
....
....
....
....
....
....
....
....
....
....
....
....
....
....
....
....
....
....

And the grace of our Lord was exceeding abundant
with faith and love which is in Christ Jesus.

1 TIMOTHY 1:14

Are you a person who enjoys surprises? Write about a time the Lord surprised you.

Great is thy faithfulness.

LAMENTATIONS 3:23

....

....

....

....

....

....

....

Have you ever thought the Lord let you down but discovered,
once you saw the full picture, that He never failed you?

....
....
....
....
....
....
....
....
....
....
....
....
....
....
....
....
....
....
....
....
....
....

As for God, his way is perfect: the word of the LORD is tried:
he is a buckler to all those that trust in him.

PSALM 18:30

....

....

....

....

....

....

When you think about God's ways being perfect, is it easier to let go of your worries? Why or why not?

For I know the thoughts that I think toward you,
saith the LORD, thoughts of peace, and not of evil,
to give you an expected end.

JEREMIAH 29:11

....
....
....
....
....
....
....
....
....
....
....
....
....

Do you believe God has given you dreams and aspirations? What dream are you focused on, and how are you pursuing it as you pursue Him?

....

....

....

....

....

....

....

....

....

....

....

....

....

....

....

....

....

....

....

....

....

And ye shall seek me, and find me, when
ye shall search for me with all your heart.

JEREMIAH 29:13

Write a prayer that tells God what it means to you when you experience His presence in a tangible way.

....

....

....

....

....

....

....

....

....

....

....

....

....

....

....

....

....

....

....

....

....

A wise man will hear, and will increase learning;
and a man of understanding shall attain unto wise counsels.

PROVERBS 1:5

Listening is a powerful communication key that unlocks the
hearts of others. What has listening done for you in your
relationships?

....

....

....

....

....

....

....

....

....

....

....

....

....

....

....

....

....

....

....

....

....

The LORD hath heard my supplication;
the LORD will receive my prayer.

PSALM 6:9

....
....
....
....
....
....

In times of prayer and intercession, you may experience a knowing that the Lord heard your prayer. How does that empower you in your faith?

....

....

....

....

....

....

....

....

....

....

....

....

....

....

....

....

....

....

....

....

....

....

Let Your Creativity Flow With. . .

Blessed: A Journal for the Highly Creative Soul

Blessed: A Journal for the Highly Creative Soul features a wonderful variety of activities to match the creative mood of the day. With an abundance of blessings-themed inspiration, dozens of delightful pages will calm with coloring; encouraging words will whisper to souls as they write; and "blank canvas" pages will inspire sketching and doodling.

Paperback / 978-1-68322-395-5 / $12.99

Best Loved Psalms Coloring Book

Color your way to an inspired faith with the *Best Loved Psalms Coloring Book*. Dozens of unique images on quality stock will uplift and encourage through beautiful design and scripture selections from the beloved King James Version of the Bible. The backs of each generous 8x10 coloring page are left blank—perfect for coloring with crayons, colored pencils, or markers.

Paperback / 978-1-68322-339-9 / $9.99